Delivered by His Power
Living in His Righteousness

Testimonies and Basic
Deliverance Teaching

by
Kathryn Sears

CONTENTS

	Forward	i
1	That They May Have Life	1
2	Lord Deliver Me!	5
3	Generational Curses	11
4	Spirits of Fear and Other Pesky Demons	15
5	Deliverance for My Husband and Children	19
6	Control Spirits	23
7	Saved by Grace and Walking in Righteousness	29
8	Satan Has Been a Liar From the Beginning	33
9	Pride Goes Before a Fall	37
10	Forgiveness is Essential	41
11	Geographical Strongholds	45
12	God Has Set Us in a Family	47
13	Keeping Your Deliverance	49
	Recommended Reading	53

Forward

I pray that my testimonies and the testimonies of others shared in this book will increase your faith and inspire you to take authority over evil spirits. As believers, we have been commissioned to do the same things Jesus did. ***John 14:12*** tells us, "Most assuredly I say to you, he who believes in Me, the works that I do he will do also; and greater works than these he will do, because I go to my Father." We also read in Isaiah how the coming Messiah (Jesus) will come to set the captives free: "The Spirit of the Lord God is upon Me, because He has anointed Me to preach good tidings to the poor; He has sent Me to heal the brokenhearted, to proclaim liberty to the captives, and the opening of the prison to those who are bound…" ***Isaiah 61:1-2.***

I sincerely believe my daughter, Naomi, would not have lived if the Lord had not brought me into the knowledge and experience of deliverance. Casting out demons was a vital part of Christ's ministry on earth. Unfortunately, the ministry of deliverance is sadly neglected today, resulting in a lack of holiness and victory in the church, and even the loss of lives. Let's believe God's word, walk in faith and expect great things. "…the people who know their God shall be strong, and carry out great exploits." ***Daniel 11:32b.***

Chapter 1

That They May Have Life

"My people are destroyed because of the lack of knowledge" *Hosea 4:6a AMP*

My hand trembled as I picked up the phone to call for an ambulance, "My baby is having trouble breathing. Send an ambulance immediately." The dispatcher started asking time consuming questions. Having already been put on hold by the pediatrician's answering service, I realized I'd better start screaming if I wanted action. "She's dying! Send an ambulance now!" I shrieked.

Our two and a half month old baby girl, Naomi, laid on the dining room table, her body limp and clammy, and her little face graying now. Even though John, her father, knew nothing about CPR, he was blowing into her lungs hoping it would help. Still fighting for her life, Naomi let out a pitiful whine each time she received air.

Just five hours earlier, our home bustled with festive activities as we hosted a Christmas party for the children who attended our Bible club. Naomi seemed under the weather, and I wondered if she was coming down with a cold. I forgot my concerns when she nursed well and fell asleep at around ten o'clock. At 2:00 a.m. I heard her whimpering and felt my husband's elbow coaxing me out of bed for her feeding. I hesitated for a few minutes, hoping she would go back to sleep but it didn't work. As I took her out of the crib, I knew she felt unusually cold. Pushing away alarming thoughts, I continued downstairs to feed her. She refused to nurse and her crying became more intense by the minute. I ran back to John, putting Naomi into his arms and practically shouting told him, "She's not hungry, she's sick! I'm going to call the doctor." John felt Naomi's head expecting to find a fever. He was shocked to discover signs of death. Her cold, pale skin sent chills of fear through both of us. Now minutes later, we had Naomi on the dining room table, where she lay lifeless and silent. I busied myself, getting dressed to go with her when the ambulance arrived. I walked and prayed, not wanting to look in her direction, for I couldn't watch my baby die. Strong, fervent prayers came easily. My usual inhibitions did not hold me back this time. As I prayed, I heard the Holy Spirit say, "spirit of death." Then John 10:10 flashed through my mind: "The thief comes only to steal and kill and destroy. I have come that they may have life, and have it to the full." With a command, I ordered that spirit of death to come out in the name of Jesus. It took only a moment, and then miraculously, Naomi began breathing.

Although she was still weak and colorless, her precious life was being restored. The doorbell rang. The paramedics had arrived and after a quick check, we were told there was no neurological damage. Rainbow Babies and Children's Hospital admitted Naomi for tests but warned she would be in the hospital four days before tests could start. The Christmas holiday meant a skeleton staff and little hope of the work being done earlier. The next morning our situation was put on a prayer chain. Only a few hours later a doctor surprised me by saying, "Well, you're very lucky, the staff involved are willing to stay and do the tests Naomi needs, and the company with the apnea monitor, which Naomi must have before leaving the hospital, is here for another case and just happened to have a spare monitor on the van. The last test is an overnighter. I suggest you go home, get a good night's sleep and pick up Naomi tomorrow morning." Gratefully, I thanked her and tried to explain it wasn't luck but the Lord working through prayer. The doctor just shrugged her shoulders and went on her way.

John and I drove back to the hospital on Christmas morning with tears of joy, knowing that if it wasn't for God's goodness, His power and love, we could have been making funeral arrangements that day. What a time of rejoicing we had that Christmas. Thank you Heavenly Father for giving Your Son so that we could enjoy our daughter. I love you so much Jesus!!!

Jesus Came to Set the Captives Free

In the 1980's my life was so dramatically impacted through deliverance (the casting out of demons) that I came to a whole new level in spiritual warfare. I learned that "… the weapons of our warfare are not carnal, but mighty through God to the pulling down of strongholds. Casting down imaginations, and every high thing that exalts itself against the knowledge of God"... ***2 Cor 10:4-5***. As Christians we are to pursue holiness, not necessarily happiness, and deliverance is part of the purification process. When we seek first the Kingdom of God and His righteousness then the love, peace and joy will follow. For far too long much of the body of Christ has been satisfied to live a mediocre Christian life, having a little victory but not worrying about the sins and so called minor addictions which seem "impossible" for them to give up. Let our hearts say with the Psalmist David: "As the deer pants for the water brooks, so pants my soul for You, O God."... ***Psalm 42:1***. Let's be discontented with status quo and seek the Lord for all He has for us. Jesus paid the highest price to redeem us from Satan's influence, sin, and deception, and has given us all we need pertaining to life and godliness.

Chapter 2

Lord Deliver Me!

I will deliver you and you will glorify Me
Palms 50:15

Eight years after my salvation experience, I still struggled with so many things that must have grieved God. I had a lot of teaching on crucifying the flesh and I really did my best to deny my ungodly desires and tried hard to be a good wife and mother. Unfortunately, all of my efforts just weren't enough. I felt like I had weights tied around my legs. This made light housework a heavy chore. It was all I could do just to take care of the "Three D's" each day: dishes, diapers and dinner. I was ashamed of my laziness and my bad temper, especially as I yelled at my 2-year old daughter, Anna. Here I am - born-again, baptized in the Holy Spirit, and yet with very little victory in these areas.

On my knees I cried out, "Lord, deliver me!" Surprised at what had come out of my mouth, I almost recanted. In 1982 we did not use the word "deliver", and as an English woman not prone to any exaggeration or strong language, I was stunned at what I had just said. But instead of recanting, I let out a determined shout, "Yes Lord, deliver me!" As things transpired in the months to come, I now have no doubt in my mind that my prayer came straight out of my heart, directly led by the Holy Spirit. Minutes after my prayer, my neighbor's daughter rang the doorbell. "My mother wants you to come over to meet Pastor Charles from our church. He is here visiting right now."

As I talked with her Pastor and asked some pertinent questions, I could see he was a man with a good knowledge of the Word of God and what he was saying made so much sense. I decided to visit his church and started to attend on Sunday nights. By the end of the first sermon I was excited, believing my bad temper could be a demon and I could actually be victorious over it. My biggest concern was the way I lost my temper with Anna. My turn for prayer came, and I explained my concern. The pastor simply said, "In the Name of Jesus, I command the spirit of bad temper to come out". The next morning when I was brushing Anna's teeth, I could tell something was different. I did not even feel tempted to yell at her when she fidgeted and pulled away. I was so happy! The following Sunday night I could hardly wait to get back in line for prayer for deliverance from laziness. In the same way Pastor Clark had commanded the spirit of bad temper to come out, he took authority over the spirit of laziness. Arriving home, I felt a burst of energy and flitted about watering house plants and cleaning up. The plants must have thought they had a new owner, because normally they wouldn't get watered until they were almost dead. I knew I was free and danced around, praising and worshipping our wonderful Lord Jesus.

About three months later, I noticed that I had a problem with nervousness. One day as I was vacuuming the stairs, my husband John walked in from work. He simply called out, "Hi, I'm home!" I screamed and the vacuum cleaner almost went flying down the stairs. Suddenly my eyes were opened to the fact this behavior was not normal, and a spirit of nervousness was causing me to act in some obsessive compulsive ways. For instance, since I was a child, cold sores would always last for months. Because I was compelled to pick the scabs, they were unable to heal. The following Sunday night I attended Freedom Chapel and got in line for ministry. "Pastor Clark, I believe I have a spirit of nerves." He commanded the spirit of nerves to come out in Jesus' Name. As he did that I heard a voice in my head. It said, "I've been here since she was seven." I had a flashback and remembered the difficult circumstances my family was going through at that time. I could see how my situation could have invited in a demon. I showed no indication of having heard a voice and there were no other manifestations; and yet Pastor Clark, through the gift of discerning of spirits, said to me: "This one is not coming out. You need to renounce it." I had never heard this term before. He instructed me to simply say, "In the Name of Jesus I renounce the spirit of nervousness." Again he commanded it to come out in Jesus name and then went on to the next person. I would not have had any way of telling whether the spirit had left me except that the next day I had a brand-new cold sore, and for the first time since I was seven years old, my cold sore was healed in eight days. I am also calmer and generally much more peaceful.

Months went by before the Lord started to reveal to me another group of spirits. I had always struggled with fantasy in the area of romance. The spirit of fantasy was manifesting itself in lustful dreams. Serious marriage problems did not help this situation. Lack of love and affection and a lack of my husband's desire for me made it more difficult to keep my thoughts toward other men pure. I cried out to God for holiness and victory in this area. I repented and battled on my knees, but saw no real change. I couldn't seem to prevent my mind from thinking evil thoughts. Wishing my husband dead was a regular occurrence. I realize now these were spirits of hate, murder and adultery in operation. I called Pastor Clark and told him what the Lord had shown to me. He told me he was going out of town and to call him in about three weeks. I thanked him and hung up. I knew I did not want to wait three weeks, knowing these demons were inside of me doing their dirty work. I fasted and prayed that day, went to a quiet place, and with all the authority I could muster, I renounced the spirits of hate, murder and adultery, and I commanded each one to come out individually in Jesus' Name. As the spirit of hate came out I felt a kind of burning sensation come up through my belly and chest and I coughed up phlegm.

When John got home that night, I saw him in a different light. It was as if I had taken off dark sunglasses and put on rose-tinted glasses. The love I had been crying out to God for had come. As he spoke unkind words to me I answered him with a gentle voice. Afterwards I asked the Lord why I had not feared him as I normally would. The Lord spoke to me by dropping a Scripture into my mind. "Perfect love casts out all fear." ***1 John 4:18***. I then realized that deliverance from the spirit of hate had given me the freedom to love my husband, and because of that love, the spirit of fear of him had to leave.

Chapter 3

Generational Curses

Christ has redeemed us from the Curse of the Law, having become a curse for us (for it is written, "Cursed is everyone who hangs on a tree")
Galatians 3:13

Upon our return from England, Pastor Charles loaned me a set of teachings by Derek Prince on deliverance and spiritual warfare. Having just found out that neither my maternal grandfather, nor my paternal grandfather could read or write, the information on generational curses was very significant. It came as revelation to me that dyslexia and other learning disabilities; I'd struggled with all my life, were curses that had come down from earlier generations. I forgave and blessed, and by faith, brought these curses to the cross and confessed them broken. It was definitely a break through. My reading and ability to learn improved. I began to apply this teaching and the breaking generational curses in other areas.

Galatians 3:10b says, "Cursed is everyone who does not continue in all things which are written in the book of the law, to do them." And verse *11* says, But that no one is justified by the law in the sight of God is evident, for "the just shall live by faith." Generally, anything we receive from the Lord is to be appropriated and received by faith and confession. If salvation, the baptism in the Holy Spirit, healing, and most other things are by faith;

then it stands to reason that we also break generational curses and ungodly soul ties by faith. Even though Jesus has already paid the price, broken the curses and healed us by His stripes, it is important to confess with our mouths and believe in our hearts as the scriptures tell us. ***Romans 10:9-10,*** "That if you confess with your mouth the Lord Jesus and believe in your heart that God has raised Him from the dead, you will be saved. For with the heart one believes unto righteousness, and with the mouth confession is made unto salvation..." Generational curses are very real and referred to in scripture numerous times. One example of this is ***Numbers 14:18***, "The LORD is longsuffering and abundant in mercy, forgiving iniquity and transgression; but He by no means clears the guilty, visiting the iniquity of the fathers on the children to the third and fourth generations."

    I have found that many people who had sudden death in their family and a lot of life threatening illnesses, have had in their bloodline some type of sin leading to death. In one instance, a friend with an autoimmune disease had a Grandfather who'd murdered a man. This brought a curse of early death and illness to come upon her bloodline. Through experience I have found that the only real remedy for the breaking of these curses is true, deep repentance and deliverance. Even if the one who committed the sin is not willing to repent, you as the Christian must do this on behalf of your relatives. You may even be led by the Lord to go to the violated family and ask for their forgiveness.

Derek Prince has brought Christian leaders together and applied these principles over cities and nations; he has seen some powerful breakthroughs. It works for cities and nations and it will work for us.

The Holy Spirit continued to give me discernment into areas in my own life related to generational curses. Still waking up from sexually immoral dreams, and feelings of guilt that lingered throughout the day, I knew there must be a way of deliverance, and I started asking the Lord what was causing these dreams. He gave me several flashbacks which brought revelation. The Lord began to teach me and revealed to me generational curses. He reminded me of things that had been said which gave me insight into the demonic control that came down through my bloodline. He taught me that in order to become free, I needed to forgive and bless all who had passed down curses. Because Jesus became a curse for us, I had to take the curses to the cross by faith. Again He showed me a specific group of spirits. I had lust, flirting and fantasy. I applied what I'd learned regarding generational curses and then took authority over these spirits and cast them out. I enjoyed a whole new freedom. Interestingly, these spirits had been causing a phenomenon which I had experienced frequently. This experience was frightening at times. Periodically, when I tried to wake up in the morning, I felt an evil presence holding me down. One morning it was particularly strong. I was trying, but with great difficulty, to speak the Name of Jesus. I had a sense that the Name of Jesus must come out of my mouth in order for me to get free. As His name started to come out with a whisper, the Lord gave me an amazing encounter. It was as if He had opened up a corner of the bedroom for me to see into the supernatural realm. As I proclaimed the name "Jesus" through the opening in my room, I heard the beautiful sound of myriads of angels singing. As the victory started to come, the singing grew louder; and when I was free, the singing faded away. Through this occurrence the Lord gave me more insight into spiritual warfare. When we call upon the name of the Lord, one way in which the angels fight for us is through praise and worship. I am so thankful for the awesome power in the name of Jesus. Surprisingly though, this incident was not the last time it happened. It wasn't until after my deliverance from the lust spirits that these demonic visitations totally stopped. Looking back, I believe the Lord allowed me to struggle in these sins for a season in order that I would not go back to them. It took a full year of periodic fasting and prayer to get free from these spirits of adultery, hate, murder, lust, flirting and fantasy. I now know these things are like spiritual rattle snakes. If you play around with them, they will eventually get you. I was determined not to get entangled again to these bondages, but to live in the glorious freedom paid for by the power of the Cross!

Chapter 4

Spirits of Fear and Other Pesky Demons

"For God hath not given us the spirit of fear; but of power, and of love, and of a sound mind."
2 Timothy 1:7

Being told I had a spirit of fear of the supernatural offended me a little. How could that be when I did spiritual warfare and cast out demons? "Okay" said my friends, "We will pray for the Lord to show you." Well, He showed me. Soon after our conversation, I had another one of my nightmares. There were dark shadows chasing me and I was full of fear. When I woke up, I believed my friends, and asked the Lord to show me how I'd opened a door for it to get in. On my knees inquiring of the Lord, I had a flashback of me as a three or four year old. I was at a seaside resort begging my father to take me on a particular ride. I didn't realize it was a ghost train and that it would scare me. The Lord brought that to my memory to deal with and get free from the spirit of fear of the supernatural. I forgave my father and blessed him in prayer, and then renounced that spirit and cast it out. Another interesting one was fear of the dark. I would always rush to the light switch. I didn't want to be in the dark for even a second. After that thing was cast out, I walked through the house without turning lights on just for fun!

A spirit of claustrophobia (or fear of enclosed and narrow places) manifested itself while

I was on a train traveling through Russia. Whatever Satan has in you, he will pull out and use against you, especially on a mission trip. I was in a small cabin with three other team members. There were two bunk beds and just enough room to stand between them. It was a very hot night and the window wouldn't open, and although I was only forty-two, I was plagued with excessive hot flashes. Then low and behold, claustrophobia raised its ugly head. By about two in the morning, I felt like I was suffocating and could not stay in that hot cubicle any longer. I was sitting outside in the corridor when one of the ladies woke up and saw me. My other roommates then woke up and started to pray for my deliverance. I asked the Lord how the claustrophobia got in, then immediately saw myself as a little girl playing with an old pram (baby carriage). Playfully, my brother rolled it over, and I was trapped underneath it, upside down. I screamed and panicked and even though I was only stuck for a few minutes before my brother got me out, apparently that was all it took for Satan to take advantage of the situation. Later, I learned my Father also has claustrophobia, and I believe it to be hereditary – making it easier for Satan to slip in. In prayer, I forgave those involved and cast that demon out. Thank you Lord!

Freedom from bondages is a wonderful thing. He has delivered me from so much. I have been set free from depression, vanity, excessive hot flashes and numerous other pesky demons. For instance, I had depression that stayed well hidden and came out only at certain times. It made me think it was a natural part of life. At age nineteen, right before I was saved, I was in deep depression and wanted to die. Becoming a Christian seemed to take care of that problem. Unfortunately though, I would get bouts of depression every month right before my menstrual cycle. I also had three months of horrible postnatal depression after the birth of my first child. Still I did not realize I was dealing with a spirit until one day when I was so down and depressed that I threw my Bible across the room. It was at that point I knew it was a demon. I cast it out and it never bothered me again. I am not always on top of the world; however, there is a difference between a spirit of depression and being a little somber.

Chapter 5

Deliverance for my Husband and Children

"As for me and my house we will serve the Lord." *Joshua 24:15*

The Lord started to lead me to do deliverance for my family. I noticed one day how my oldest daughter could not speak to family friends without looking very nervous. She was only three years old and quite shy. She would put her hand in her mouth and not look into their faces. After taking authority over the spirit of nerves in her, she became much more relaxed; so obviously the spirit of nerves had left her. Similarly, my second daughter Rachel, a beautiful two year old, suddenly became extremely rebellious. When I called her she would go the other way. Verbally she was showing no respect and was generally very stubborn. I dealt with this for about six weeks. I prayed and realized it was a spirit of rebellion. The Lord also revealed to me how it had gotten in. As we were saving up to go on a trip back to England, her father had been working many hours of overtime. Alone with the children day after day, I had become irritable. My care toward them was not as loving and gentle as it should have been. This opened the door for Rachel to be vulnerable to the spirit of rebellion. I repented of my behavior. One night after a situation with Rachel, where she was very disobedient and disrespectful, I spanked her; but it did not help her attitude. I realized that this was the time to command the spirit out. Minutes

19

before this, I had asked Rachel if she wanted Jesus in her heart. She yelled very stubbornly, "No!" After commanding the demon out, her countenance changed. She looked relieved and happy. I asked her once again, "Do you want Jesus in your heart?" Jumping up and down, she said, "Yes! Yes!" After asking Jesus into her heart, she was so excited she ran into my bedroom and started jumping on the bed. Unfortunately she jumped forward and hit her lip on the headboard. Even though I was using ice to try to stop the bleeding, blood poured from her mouth and wouldn't stop. I called a friend to agree with me in prayer and immediately the wound started to close up. What a mighty God we serve! A few weeks later we departed for our month long vacation visiting family in England. Anna and Rachel were well behaved and a tremendous witness to everyone we came into contact with.

Even though that trip was so amazing in many ways, it was one of the toughest months of my life. Every time the Lord wanted us to move in a certain direction, my husband John said no, and I would go into the bathroom just to pray in tongues. John was being very difficult and oppressive, but the devil was not able to stop what God was doing. My Grandmother got saved, and a few weeks later went to be with the Lord. My cousin's wife received the baptism in the Holy Spirit and my sister-in-law was healed of Placenta Previa. Nevertheless, arriving home, I felt the heavy weight of hurt and rejection. As I cried out to the Lord, He spoke to me very clearly and said, "If you would fast and pray for your husband like you do for everyone else, Satan wouldn't be able to use him like he does." With that said, I went on a five day water fast. A scripture which has always encouraged me in fasting has been **Matthew 17:14–21**. When the disciples could not cast the demon out of a young man, they asked Jesus why not. In verse 20 the Lord said, "Because of your unbelief..." and in verse 21 "However, this kind does not go out except by prayer and fasting." I believe fasting, coupled with prayer, worship and the word of God, builds our faith and positions us to "be strong and carry out great exploits" **Dan 11:32b**. On my five day fast, the Lord told me to come against the fear of man and pride in my husband. By the end of that fast, there was a significant difference in him and for the next four or five years he was much easier to live with. However, the last time I tried to fast for my husband, the Lord told me He would not take away his freedom again. Within a year, I saw John's heart completely harden toward God and towards me. Sadly, our marriage of twenty one years ended in divorce.

Chapter 6

Control Spirits, 1 Kings 16 – 2 Kings 9

1 and 2 Kings details the life and character of Jezebel, who is the picture of wickedness, and was used by Satan to bring a lot of trouble down on Israel. Through murder, idolatry, manipulation and sexual perversion, she took things into her own hands and controlled a nation. Of course she came to a violent end and received her just reward. The book of ***Revelation 2:20-23*** refers to her. Most likely Jezebel is not the real name of the ungodly woman in the church at Thyatira. I believe the Lord is referring to this person as having the spirit of Jezebel. The Spirit of the Lord is totally the opposite to the spirit of Jezebel, and as Christians we must endeavor to display character and fruitfulness as far away from this spirit as heaven is from hell.

Through years of women's ministry I have found myself working with all kinds of personalities. Some ladies have been very easy and a pleasure to work with, and others more of a challenge. I found myself bending over backwards trying to please everyone. The ones who were controlling were never satisfied. When I realized I was being more and more careful to do everything they wanted so as not to cause trouble, I knew I was quenching the Holy Spirit and I needed some deliverance in this area.

Quite early on in my walk with the Lord, I had strong Christian women in my life who seemed very loving and caring; but, who wanted to tell me what to do and how to run my life. I felt obligated to reciprocate that love by visiting and calling them on a regular basis. After I was married, they tried to control my husband through me. Through situations like these, the Lord was teaching me more about the spirit realm. It wasn't the ladies that were my problem, but the demons both in me and them. "For we do not wrestle against flesh and blood, but against principalities, against powers, against the rulers of the darkness of this age, against spiritual hosts of wickedness in the heavenly places." ***Ephesian 6:12.*** Yes, some of these ladies had control spirits; however, they would not have been able to control me if I hadn't had a spirit of fear of man and a people-pleasing spirit. In order to control, the Jezebel (or control spirit) always needs someone with Ahab type spirits (primarily spirits of fear and timidity). Once I gained the victory in this area and broke free, I was able to speak the truth in love, minister more freely, and with more confidence. Nevertheless, the ladies with the control spirits, whether consciously or unconsciously, were still trying to close down the ministry I led. Soon afterwards they resigned and the Lord blessed me with a godly group of women leaders.

It came as quite a surprise to me; however, to find I too had a control spirit. This became apparent when, for about a year, I fostered troubled children. I was not allowed to spank them and pretty soon they just did what they liked. I tried to get them to behave properly by yelling. That didn't work and just made me feel guilty. I felt constantly agitated by their lying, stealing and disrespectful attitudes. I was so distraught by my lack of capacity to respond in love to these children, and for months I cried out to God, "Lord what does Satan have in me that gives the demons in these children the ability to upset me?" I so wanted to be a good witness to them. The Lord answered me and said, "Control". He showed me I was trying to control them – trying to make them act right. Years before this, knowing of the unhealthy control my Grandmother had over her family, I had renounced the spirit of control when going through what I call systematic deliverance. Apparently it didn't work. I now realize the Lord often has to bring us to the point of desperation before we can get true deliverance. Due to the fact that I was such a failure as a foster parent, the Lord had my full attention. He made me realize at that moment I had to relinquish all control to Him. I had to give complete control into His hands. I did some self-deliverance and released the children to God. It was my job to love them, and set and enforce guidelines. The peace that came through relinquishing all control to the Lord was amazing.

I knew a man who although fearful, appeared very confident and in charge. He had a control spirit that was fueled by fear and pride. He would go to great lengths to hide his true self from the people around him. When he'd been at a church for a while he would pull away; stop going to the mid-week service and stop letting his wife invite people over. He feared close friendships with Christians, as they may realize he didn't love God. He feared closeness to God thinking God would ask him to do something embarrassing such as witness to an unsaved person. In many ways this man's control spirit affected his wife and children. For six years, at his request, his wife did not drive, and he was not in a hurry to take her to the places she needed to go. He restricted his children's participation in extracurricular activities and discouraged prayer and Bible reading, hindering growth in most areas of their lives. One person's control spirit affects not just their lives but can affect generations to come.

    Over bearing and over protective parents are actually operating under a control spirit. Too often in our American society adult children are treated like twelve year olds. Parents who are always bailing their children out and protecting them from ever suffering the consequences of their actions are not doing them any favors. These Christian parents are crying out to God for their children, and yet seem to be oblivious to the fact that they are doing everything possible to stop God from disciplining them. They pay their fines, pay their bills, they make their phone calls to plan their lives, and then wonder why their adult children never grow up to be responsible, productive citizens. We see in *2 Samuel 15* how Absalom, the son King David spoiled, became rebellious and stirred up Israel against his Father David. The same is true today. If a child is spoiled or not raised to be responsible, that child will cause trouble for his/her parents and many other people around them.

Dear body of Christ I implore you, if you see in yourself a tendency to control, please fast, pray and repent. Control is one of Satan's characteristics and his only aim is to kill, steal and destroy. Control will sap us of confidence and inhibit creativity and growth. If we love those around us we will want to enhance their giftings and pray for a way to encourage healthy growth, and control will never do that. Give the control to the Lord and see what God will do! True love allows people to make mistakes, and it is humble and not proud.

Chapter 7

Saved by Grace and Walking in Righteousness

Deliverance and holiness doesn't always come easily. The struggle for holiness can be a long road, but we must keep walking. We must deny ourselves of anything that would lead to ungodliness. The victory is promised. "But thanks be to God who gives us the victory through Jesus Christ our Lord." *1 Cor 15:57.* If we live in defeat and become content with our sin, we are denying the power of the cross. Let's live the life Jesus died to give us. "…who Himself bore our sins in His own body on the tree, that we, having died to sins, might live for righteousness"… *1 Peter 2:24.* *Hebrews 5:7-8* tells us, "Jesus who in the days of His flesh, when He had offered up prayers and supplications, with vehement cries and tears to Him who heard because of His godly fear, though He was a Son, yet He learned obedience by the things which He suffered." If Jesus had to learn obedience by the things He suffered, why should we think we can sail through life without a fight? We read in *Luke 22:42* and *44* how Jesus called out to His Father: "Father if it is your will, take this cup from me; nevertheless not My will, but Yours be done." And being in agony, he prayed more earnestly". Then His sweat became like great drops of blood falling down to the ground." *2 Corinthians 7:1* "Therefore, having these promises, beloved, let us **cleanse ourselves from all filthiness of the flesh and spirit,** perfecting holiness in the fear of God."

We know that our own righteousness cannot save, heal or deliver us. All of the dying to self, and self-abasement could never lead to a place in heaven. It is only through knowing Jesus, trusting in His finished work on the cross and the shed blood of the Son of God as payment for our sins. In this way, we can be saved from eternal death and hell. ***Ephesians 2:8-9*** "For by grace you have been saved through faith, and that not of yourselves; it is the gift of God, not of works, lest anyone should boast." It is so clear in Scripture that our salvation does not depend on how good we are and yet we have numerous exhortations to "be good". This can seem so confusing. I like to look at it this way: Because we are in covenant with God through Jesus blood, He has given us everything we need to gain the victory and glorify Him. He has given us His word, power in His name; the baptism in the Holy Spirit, angelic assistance, intercession, the knowledge of His awesome love - and so the benefits go on and on. Consequently, in the same way that we would not want to commit adultery against our spouse, or hurt those we love, so we would not want to commit spiritual adultery against our Lord who we are betrothed to as our heavenly Bridegroom. If we truly love Him, we will delight in blessing Him and becoming pure in His sight.

Our motivation for getting rid of demons should be our love for God. That love is propelling us to want to be pure and Holy for our Lord. The first commandment is to "Love the Lord your God with all your heart, with all your soul, and with all your strength." ***Deut 6:5***. There are so many reasons why some people go through deliverance. For example, when a person becomes a Christian, it's no longer cool to smell like cigarette smoke. Some want deliverance because the demons are causing pain, discomfort or fear. Praise the Lord, because whatever the reason, many times even when we come to Him with wrong motives we get freedom from those unwanted and ungodly bondages. God is merciful! However, if your purpose is not primarily your love for God and to be a clean vessel for Him, then please spend time falling in love with your Lord once again. ***1 John 4:19*** tells us, "We love Him because He first loved us." Nurture your love for Him. Sing to Him, talk to Him, read His word back to Him. First, 2nd and 3rd John are all about His love for us and how we should love each other. Pursue Jesus with all of your heart!

Chapter 8

Satan Has Been a Liar From the Beginning

"...that serpent of old, called Devil and Satan, who deceives the whole world..."
Revelation 12:9

Even though there are times when deliverance from demons happens sovereignly, for the most part, they will need to be cast out. We rejoice with those who go down under the power of the Holy Spirit and come up totally healed and delivered. Still, we must be vigilant, knowing Satan is a deceiver and hides himself well. Obviously, with many excuses and reasons, Satan will try to talk you out of getting rid of demons. Down through the years I've heard Christians say, "Well I went through deliverance at such and such church, so if there was anything in me it's out now and I'm clean." Unfortunately, that is not usually the case. If there is still fear, lust, accidents, infirmities and such in operation in that person's life then they are simply being deceived by Satan. One man told me he "wasn't into this deliverance stuff". He had just read the book I'd given him by Heidi Baker and felt that a Christian's focus should be on loving the poor. Regrettably, the spirits of rejection and abandonment prohibited him from loving, and caused him to be very easily offended. These spirits were hindering the love of the Lord from flowing through him to others. Praise the Lord, he did eventually get some deliverance.

Similarly, I have a friend who thought the message of grace was the way to deliverance from depression. Yes, teachings reminding us we don't have to perform to earn God's love are very freeing; nevertheless if the depression is caused by a demon the relief may only be temporary. Demons, or spirits, may hide for a while, but still need to be cast out. I've heard numerous Christians say deliverance comes through reading and declaring the Word of God. Yes we are cleansed by the washing of the word. The word of God is vital "part" of our deliverance. Another brother listened to the devil quote Scripture to him. He didn't want deliverance because the devil had convinced him that when the house was swept clean, the demons that left would go and find their brothers and come back; causing his condition to be worse than before. Of course the Lord was talking about people who did not have a heart for God. After many years of straddling the fence, that brother eventually hardened his heart, walked away from the Lord and caused great damage to come to his family. If that brother had sought the Lord and become hot for God, things would have turned out so differently. Don't let the devil lie to you! The Bible warns us not to be lukewarm. ***Rev 3:15, 16 & 19***: "I know your deeds, that you are neither cold nor hot; I wish that you were cold or hot. So because you are lukewarm, and neither hot nor cold, I will spit you out of My mouth…Those whom I love, I reprove and discipline; therefore be zealous and repent."

Why do so many of God's people have such a difficult time with the concept of deliverance? Is it because of pride and fear? We don't want to admit that a filthy demon may have taken up residence in us. Some ministers are so afraid of offending their people that they command demons to come off instead of out. If you see anywhere in Scripture demons being commanded off, please tell me. I have not seen it.

Unfortunately, there are pastors who are teaching their congregations that they can never expect to have victory over sin. These pastors are most likely walking in sin themselves and Satan has them deceived and is using them to lead many astray. They are blind guides leading the blind. In **Galatians 5:18-21**, the Apostle Paul lists some of the works of the flesh: "adultery, fornication, uncleanness, lewdness, idolatry, sorcery, hatred, contentions, jealousies, outbursts of wrath, selfish ambitions, dissensions, heresies, envy, murders, drunkenness, revelries, and the like… those who practice such things will not inherit the kingdom of God." **Galatians 5:24** says, "And those who are Christ's have crucified the flesh with its passions and desires." We are in Christ Jesus, walking according to the Spirit, not the flesh. **Romans 6:4** says "Therefore we were buried with Him through baptism into death, that just as Christ was raised from the dead by the glory of the Father, even so we also should walk in newness of life." Does this mean we have to be perfect to go to heaven? No! It means we are a work in progress. Do not let the devil put fear on you. Remember, he is a liar. As a new Christian, I was quite sinful. I did not have victory over bad temper, lustful thoughts, laziness and addictions. However, I was covered with the same robe of righteousness as a mature Christian who has been raised in a Christian home and has enjoyed the benefits of a bloodline of generations of Christians. They may not have the same struggles as I did. But, if we had been walking together and were both hit by a car and died, do you think I would have gone to hell and them to heaven? No! Nevertheless, even though I still had demons in me and so little victory, I hated my sin and truly cried out to God for forgiveness and purity. I was like a toddler learning how to walk and obey mom and dad. Now in the natural, a teenager does not dirty his pants or continuously spill food on the floor nor behave rebelliously without some serious consequences. Likewise, we are not to stay spiritual toddlers. If, I truly love God, I will want to please Him and my obedience to Him will bear the fruit of righteousness.

Chapter 9

Pride Goes Before a Fall

A man's pride will bring him down low…
Proverbs 29:23a.

If a spirit of pride enters into a person, it will hold the door open for all kinds of spirits of deception. When I lived in England in the 1970's, my husband and I belonged to a wonderful Christian fellowship that suddenly turned sour. We were a congregation of about 40 people who loved God and loved one another. Our praise to the Lord was awesome, and we flowed in the gifts of the Holy Spirit. That fellowship truly was like a taste of heaven. Regretfully that changed one day when our little church fellowship met up with a church that was cultic in nature and doctrine. Our leadership had the maturity and Bible knowledge to know better, but instead they embraced it all. They saw a morsel that was tasty and attractive. The main thrust and teaching of this cultic group was dying to self; crucifying the flesh to become like Jesus. Sounds good doesn't it? Except that we had to stop enjoying praise and worship and start singing songs written about dying to self, put to tunes taken from old hymns. We wore drab clothing; kept our hair long and tied back in a scarf. Married couples were not allowed to use contraceptives and were having one baby after another. The church meetings became more like brainwashing sessions that constantly reminded us to humble ourselves to the point we were to be used as door mats. It was pretty depressing! After three years of this, the cult leaders came right out and said, "Our salvation has nothing to do with Jesus dying on the cross. We are only saved by dying to self and crucifying the flesh. By doing this you may become good enough to be saved." They taught that they were the five virgins in Jesus' parable who are raptured and the other five left behind are the rest of the born-again believers.

Being a Christian for only a few of years, I did not understand what had happened to our joyful little band of believers. I knew nothing about demonology or spiritual warfare. All I knew was that I was miserable and now didn't know if I would ever be good enough to make it to heaven. As I cried out and asked God if I was saved, He spoke to me through Scriptures: ***Romans 4:3***"Abraham believed God, and it was accounted to him for righteousness."… And, ***Romans 4:7*** "Blessed are those whose lawless deeds are forgiven, and whose sins are covered; blessed is the man to whom the Lord shall not impute sin."

Finally we got out of that cultic church; however, I was confused for years, wondering how such a good Christian fellowship could change like that and so quickly. Little by little, the Lord showed me what had happened. Because our fellowship flowed so beautifully in praise and spiritual gifts, the leadership had become proud, opening a door for the spirits of pride and deception. In the beginning most of the church knew we were off balance and in error. Some people left, but most stayed. I didn't understand how the majority, knowing something was very wrong, had no problem going along with it. Years later, my eyes were opened to what had happened. Those who stayed chose to conform in order to be accepted, not realizing that in doing so they were seeking man's approval rather than God's, and therefore guilty of a form of idolatry. They gave up the truth for a lie and became deceived. Those of us who stood up for the truth were ostracized and told, "You just have not received the revelation." Unfortunately, the church in question is still cultic and is bearing no fruit for the kingdom of Heaven.

If you are in a church where something seems odd, it probably is odd. Too often we question ourselves, thinking we must be wrong. You think, "If everyone else is okay with this then why am I concerned?" Allow your spiritual alarm to do its job. Do not agree with error in order to fit in. Speak the truth in love even if it means losing friends and being thought less of. You have a calling on your life and a destiny to fulfill. Please do not miss what the Lord has for you. Even knowing the word of God is no guarantee that we will not fall into error. The spirit of pride is so strong and blinding. We have to humble ourselves, casting out all forms of pride and deception. Love the Lord; love His word; fast, pray and take good counsel.

Chapter 10

Forgiveness is Essential

"Therefore, confess your sins to one another, and pray for one another so that you may be healed." *James 5:16a.*

Often deliverance and inner healing go hand in hand with physical healing. My friend, who I will call Anne, told me of her ministry experience with a lady we will call Jane. Jane was in the hospital dying of cancer. She shared with Anne her horrendous experience. As a young child she was playing with her twin sister when a man ran into the barn and brutally raped and murdered her twin. Jane was able to get away only to have the trauma haunt her for many years. She lived with hate and unforgiveness eating away at her, which had taken its toll on her physical body. Our Lord ministered to a woman in the temple with a spirit (demon) who had been bent over for eighteen years. He didn't judge her. It seems to me that He very lovingly laid hands on her and healed her. All Jesus had to say was, *"Woman, you are loosed from your infirmity."* ***Luke 13:10-13.*** And the spirit came out. My friend led Jane in prayers forgiving and blessing the perpetrator, and then she took authority over the spirits of hate, unforgivness, bitterness, death and cancer. Jane got free, recovered and lived. Not all cancer patients have unforgiveness, but it is something to look into when praying for healing.

During one of my visits to Ghana, we went to a school just outside Accra. The evangelistic service went well and most of the young people made commitments to Jesus. We stayed for a while to pray for the staff and teachers when suddenly there was a commotion. We were called to another part of the school where six of the teenagers were manifesting demons. Isaac, my host, interpreter and associate Pastor of a local Methodist church, had a lot of experience in this area and jumped right in there along with several of the Christian teachers. For about two hours they yelled, "Come out in the name of Jesus!" I assumed they knew what they were doing and stood at the side of the room praying in tongues and covering everyone with Jesus blood. It seemed that we had some victory. For the most part, the girls had stopped screaming, running around and rolling on the dirt floor. Obviously some of them had gotten a measure of deliverance; still, there was a ways to go. I sensed the Holy Spirit prompt me to go to each one and gently remind them how much Jesus loved them, how much He suffered and died for them; and to lead them in forgiving the girl who had gotten them involved in the occult. One of the girls would not forgive; thankfully, the others did forgive and became free. When the demons started manifesting in one precious little thirteen year old, they struck her dumb. My heart went out to her as she lay on the ground looking so helpless. I got down on the ground next to her, and I asked her if she really wanted to be delivered and wanted Jesus to be Lord of her life. She responded to my questions by nodding or writing in the dirt. She gave her life to the Lord and forgave those who had done her harm. I then commanded the spirits to come out in the name of Jesus and helped her up. In freedom she gave thanks and praise to the Lord. This incident reminded me of **Luke 11:14**, "And He (Jesus) was casting out a demon, and it was mute. So it was, when the demon had gone out, that the mute spoke..." Thank you Lord for your love and power!

We were invited back one week later, and I taught on the Baptism in the Holy Spirit. Just as the anointing fell and the young people had started to receive, I heard screaming coming from the back of the auditorium. I knew it was the girl who had refused to forgive and had not been delivered from the evil spirits. Isaac immediately sprang into action and was about to rush to the girl to do deliverance. I caught his arm and said, "No! Leave her alone, it is not the time for that. The devil is trying to stop what the Holy Spirit is doing here." Through the microphone with Isaac interpreting, I explained, "The devil is just trying to distract us." A couple of teachers took the young lady out and then the holy hush returned. The Holy Spirit continued His work and many of the children and teenagers received the Baptism in the Holy Spirit with tongues and tears. It was a glorious time. I have not been back to that school since, but I pray the young lady did forgive and did get her deliverance also.

Chapter 11

Geographical Strongholds

"Seek the welfare of the city where I have sent you into exile, and pray to the Lord on its behalf; for in its welfare you will have welfare." Or some versions say, "in its peace you shall have peace."
Jeremiah 29:7

There was always trouble on our street and things were getting worse. Three home owners had rented out their places to large inner city families with a lot of problems. If your stuff wasn't screwed down it would get stolen; and sometimes it would even get unscrewed and then stolen. Three times as friends left our home, they went out of the door only to find their cars had disappeared. Hardly a week passed by without the police being called. I fasted and prayed for the salvation of our neighbors and invited the neighborhood children to our Bible club. Some of them came and received the Lord. All of the children had come into my home at some time or another for milk and cookies. The summer was a tough one. I was the only mother at home during the day. I found myself breaking up fights and trying to keep the peace. Finally, I really felt like I'd had enough. The ladies Bible study I hosted in my home prayed fervently. The Lord had given us revelation that it was actually a spirit or stronghold of trouble over the street. Together we cried out to the Lord and commanded that spirit to leave. It left and for many years this street has been wonderfully peaceful. Don't let Satan tell you that you can't make a difference in your area. "The effective, fervent prayer of a righteous man avails much." ***James 5:16b***. If we as Christians are praying and fasting and claiming our communities for Christ, taking authority over principalities and powers as Scripture tells us to - then the neighborhoods we live in should eventually be marked with love, joy and peace.

Chapter 12

God Has Set Us in a Family

Love one another with brotherly affection (as members of one family) ***Romans 12:10 b.***

Even though God wants us to go to Him first, He also has given us each other, the body of Christ. Do not let pride or shame stop you from asking brothers and sisters in Christ to pray for you. The Lord wants us to know that we not only need Him, we also need His people. Initially He taught me that I didn't always have to run to a ministry to have demons cast out. He wanted me to see that I have the authority and should use it. However, God never wants us to be Lone Rangers. He desires that the body of Christ be like a symphony orchestra, flowing together to make a beautiful melodic sound. Needing help ensures that we walk in humility. One example of this was about three months after my freedom from bad temper. I thought it may have come back although it didn't seem the same as before. I tried commanding it out and saw no change. Going back to the deliverance ministry, I sat with one of the counselors who discerned it to be a spirit of anger. She cast it out of me and more freedom came. Hallelujah! Many times I have gone to a friend or to a deliverance ministry for help, agreement in prayer and discernment. It is imperative for us to work together as a team. Not only is this more effective, but love and unity in the body of Christ glorifies God.

Chapter 13

Keeping Your Deliverance

"And they overcame him by the blood of the Lamb and by the word of their testimony..."
Revelations 12:11

"No temptation has overtaken you except such as is common to man; but God is faithful, who will not allow you to be tempted beyond what you are able, but with the temptation will also make the way of escape, that you may be able to bear it". ***1 Corinthians 10:13***. We keep our deliverance by faith, believing He is the one who keeps us and protects us. As long as we do not purposely go back to sin, we are under His covering. We serve the Almighty God. Remember the devil's power pales dramatically compared to our all-powerful Lord. Speak the Word of God out loud. Declaring and proclaiming the truth will dispel the darkness and deception. If you feel the demons trying to come back, remind them whose you are, and that you are covered with the blood of Jesus.

We now have a number of 'Freedom Centers' in our area and I recommend them to you. These are places we can go to if we need help with deliverance. Furthermore, I recommend 'Warfare Plus Ministries' website. This website has an abundance of information and testimonies. You'll gain insight and enjoy their faith-building true stories.

Church on the North Coast
www.churchonthenorthcoast.org
Lorain Campus: 4125 Leavitt Rd. Lorain, OH 44053
(440) 960-1100

Church on the Summit
8870 Brookpark Rd, Cleveland, OH 44129
(216) 741-5683

Bethel Cleveland
www.BethelCleveland.com
Freedom Center
16670 Bagley Rd, Cleveland, OH 44130
(440) 243-9001

Warfare Plus Ministries
Paul and Clair Hollis
3457 W Kenyon Ave
Tampa, FL 33614
(813) 935-4673

In closing, because Jesus paid the price on the cross, and gave us His authority, we can walk in full assurance of faith.

Colossians 2:15 Speaks of Jesus's work on the cross and tells us that "Having disarmed principalities and powers, He made a public spectacle of them, triumphing over them in it. "Behold, I give you the authority to trample on serpents and scorpions, and over all the power of the enemy, and nothing shall by any means hurt you... " ***Luke 10:19.***

God's Word is true! If He said it, I believe it! And He said, "These signs will follow those who believe; **In my name they will cast out demons**; they will speak with new tongues; they will take up serpents; and if they drink anything deadly, it will by no means hurt them; they will lay hands on the sick, and they will recover." ***Mark 16:17 & 18***

So, my dear brothers and sisters in Christ, run the race, and as the Amplified Bible says, "Never lag in zeal and in earnest endeavor; be aglow and burning with the Spirit, serving the Lord." ***Romans 12:11.***

Recommended Reading

The Bible

Pigs in the Parlor
by Frank Hammond

The Hidden Power in Prayer and Fasting
by Mahesh Chavda

They Shall Expel Demons:
What You Need to Know about Demons--
Your Invisible Enemies
by Prince, Derek

Healing through Deliverance:
The Foundation and Practice of
Deliverance Ministry
by Peter J. Horrobin and Derek Prince

Blessing or Curse:
You Can Choose
by Prince, Derek and Chavda, Mahesh

Fasting: Opening the Door to a Deeper,
More Intimate, More Powerful
Relationship With God
by Franklin, Jentezen

About The Author

Kathryn E. Sears was born and raised in England, where in her teens she was born again and Baptized in the Holy Spirit. In 1979 she relocated to the United States and started a children's bible club in her home. She also hosted Bible studies, prayer meetings, and organized evangelistic outreaches in her local community and in nursing homes. Soon after, she became president of a local women's Aglow chapter. During this same time, she started to travel internationally, taking the Word and the love of God through testimony, teaching and humanitarian aid. In the last 18 years she has ministered in the Ukraine, Haiti, Guinea, and numerous times in Russia, Cuba, Ghana and Liberia. Her mission trips have taken her out of the country over thirty times. She is now the Director of Word and Deed Ministries, which was establish in 2005 out of her passion to follow her calling to the nations. For the past five years the Lord has led her to the interior of several countries in West Africa. There, she and her team go from village to village showing the Jesus movie and leading hundreds to Christ. Also, in the power of Jesus' name, they have seen healings, deliverances and lives wonderfully changed. Kathryn is the author of three booklets: Saved by His Grace, Empowered by the Holy Spirit and Delivered by His Power.

Made in the USA
Lexington, KY
12 November 2019